Shoo, Spider!

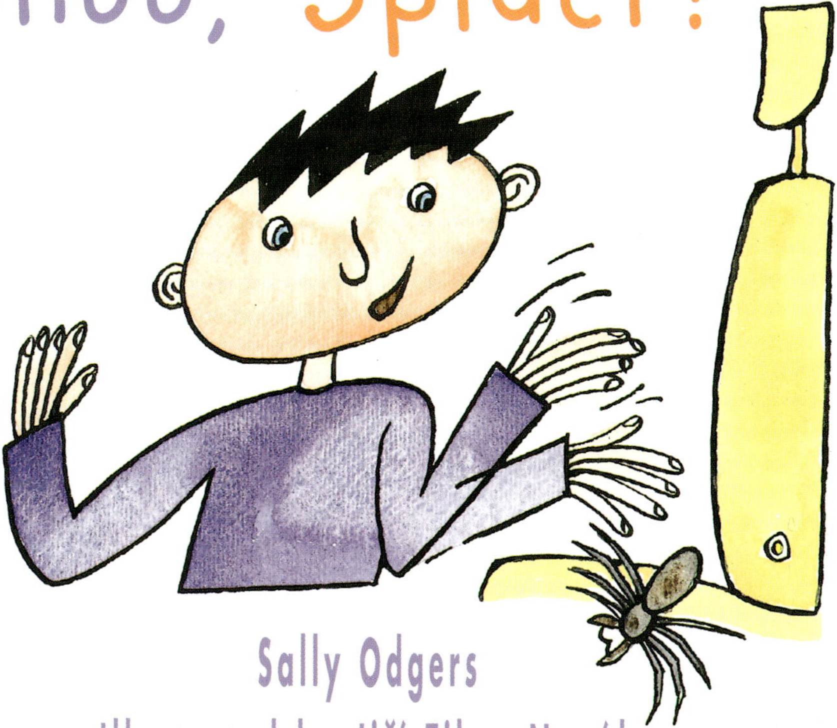

Sally Odgers
Illustrated by Jiří Tibor Novák

Patrick saw a spider in the car.
It was a big, brown spider.

The spider sat on the steering wheel.
"Oops!" said Patrick. "Mom won't like that."
It was right where Mom would put her hand.
Mom would be scared.

Shoo, spider!

Patrick brushed the spider off the steering wheel.

3

It landed on the driver's seat.
"Oops!" said Patrick. "Mom won't like that."
It was right where Mom would sit.
Mom would be scared.

Patrick brushed the spider off the seat.

It landed on the floor and ran under the seat.

"Mom won't like that," said Patrick.
"That spider could go anywhere!"

Patrick asked Dad for help.

"There's a spider in the car."

"It ran under the seat," said Patrick.
"Mom won't like that. Mom will be scared."
Dad wanted to help.

"I'll get it out. Show me where it is."

Dad looked under the seat of the car.

"Are you sure there is a spider in the car?" asked Dad.

The spider had climbed up on the roof of the car.
It was hanging upside down.

"It will drop on Mom's head if we leave it there," said Patrick.
"Mom won't like that. Mom will be scared."

"Give me the dustpan," said Dad.
"I'll move that spider."
"Don't hurt it," said Patrick.
"I won't," said Dad.
"I just want it out of the car."

Dad tried to sweep the spider
into the dustpan.
The spider fell off the roof of the car.
It landed on Dad's head.

"I don't like having a spider on my head!"
said Dad.
Dad sat in the car. His face was a funny color.

Mom came out of the house.
"What's the matter?" asked Mom.
"There's a spider in the car," said Patrick.

Mom swept the spider off Dad's head.
She put it on the ground.

The spider ran off and climbed a tree.
"Goodbye, spider," said Patrick. "Thanks, Mom."